# THE WIDOW ROADMAP

## Finding My Way

Written & Illustrated by

# Kate Seidman

Flint Hills Publishing

The Widow Roadmap – Finding My Way
© Kate Seidman 2023
All rights reserved.

Original illustrations by the author.

Cover Design by Amy Albright

stonypointgraphics.weebly.com

## Flint Hills Publishing

Topeka, Kansas
Tucson, Arizona
www.flinthillspublishing.com

Printed in the U.S.A.

Paperback Book: ISBN 978-1-953583-64-2
Hardback Book ISBN 978-1-953583-66-6
Electronic Book ISBN 978-1-953583-65-9

# CONTENTS

## Chapter 1
# My Story

*Falling in love is like seeing the ocean for the first time when all your life you've been stepping in puddles.*
Riina Nath

# Meeting Mitch

The quick version:

We met at a dancing party

on a Saturday night

on Parker Street

in Berkeley, California.

Mitch was 27                    I was 24

Kate Seidman

# The Dance

Strangers…

Sway…touch…hold…left…right…around and through.

As we move together, the steps reveal familiarity.

The dance takes me home. Days long ago forgotten.

Awake.

Who is this man who knows my hidden secrets?

I didn't even know his name.

We are the correct size and proportion.

I fit easily under his arm as he turns me.

He leads, I follow,

on and on, over and again.

We are falling

With every step

In love.

## THE WIDOW ROADMAP

Saturday night turned into Easter Sunday.

The party moved to Lands Ends

beach in San Francisco.

On the beach we watched drag queens

enact the resurrection of Christ

as the sun arrived marking a new day.

It marked the start of our relationship.

From the beginning Mitch and I had energy and passion.

We dated—broke up for 4 years—dated again

and got married.

I was 29                              Mitch was 33

We decided to leave Berkeley and move to

Gloucester where Mitch grew up.

Our choice to live on the East Coast made

both our families very happy.

I was 5 months pregnant.

We lived by the beach.

Over the next 11 years we had three beautiful children.

Aaron born January 14, 1979
Noah born June 28, 1983
Sasha born August 10, 1988

My brother Gene made this 6-foot collage of Mitch. It hung in my living room window for a year.

We were married for 33 years
No more—no less.
Of course, we had our regular fights
Mostly about time—
I didn't care while Mitch cared too much.
We had a date night,
hired a babysitter when the kids were little,
and when they got old enough
we just went out.
We cooked and ate.
We worked and danced.
We even got to travel—Mexico, Italy, Vietnam.
We watched our children grow up
and leave home one by one.
We loved them and raised them well.

I was 63                    Mitch was 66

Our friends invited us to an early birthday dinner.

"The *steak au poivre* is delicious," Mitch said, as he took another bite.

Later, in the middle of the night, Mitch started throwing up. "Kate, I think I have the flu," he complained as he crept back into bed. By morning he was untouchable, the most miserable I'd ever seen him. His backed ached, his skin was itchy, he was jaundiced, and his blue eyes were yellow.

Mitch put his symptoms into his computer…up came—

PANCREATIC CANCER.

He called his doctor who immediately got him an appointment with a surgeon.

We left Gloucester the next morning—destination…

MASS GENERAL HOSPITAL

# It was October 7th—Mitch's 66th Birthday.

The whole thing was a big mistake. We were just going to meet the surgeon and go home. But the surgeon said to us, "Mitch, stay overnight and we'll do a biopsy in the morning."

That afternoon we went to Legal Sea Foods to celebrate his birthday. I sat as close to him as I could but couldn't touch him, he was too itchy, he ate nothing.

We returned to the hospital and checked in.

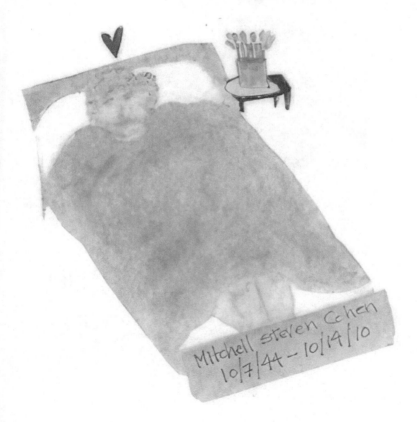

Mitchell steven Cohen
10/7/44 – 10/14/10

Kate Seidman

# The Next Morning

Just as the surgeon promised, they took a tiny sliver of
Mitch's pancreas.
Immediately he was sicker than he'd been.
The doctors couldn't control his bile
and they said he was
*underwater.*

Now we were stuck in the hospital system.

I felt like we were in the jaws of the monster.

**"They're going to kill me in here."**

**That was the last thing Mitch
ever said to me...**

**Aaron called his younger siblings,
"Come home, NOW!"**

**Our family met with the doctors. They said
it was time to take him off life support.**

**How was it possible? We just came for a
consultation with a surgeon...**

**Only one week after we entered the
hospital,**

**the doctors unhooked Mitch and shortly
after, they pronounced him dead.**

**October 14, 2010**

Standing in these colors
Howling
Screaming
Sorrow
Here in these colors
If I could scream loud enough
I can almost reach
Mitch

Kate Seidman

The next morning
I was the only one up.
I made coffee.
I looked out my window
at the ocean.

The world was showing itself to me anew.

The sun was shining brightly on the water
The air was electric—
The contrast between the beauty before me
And the loneliness within me was overpowering.

I began to cry

I knew nothing would ever be the same again.

## Away

Death came to our house
swallowing up, taking away
my husband, my children's father.

without him
I am cold
I follow
the sun
around the house

the sun
promises
to keep
me warm

I watch at
the waters
edge

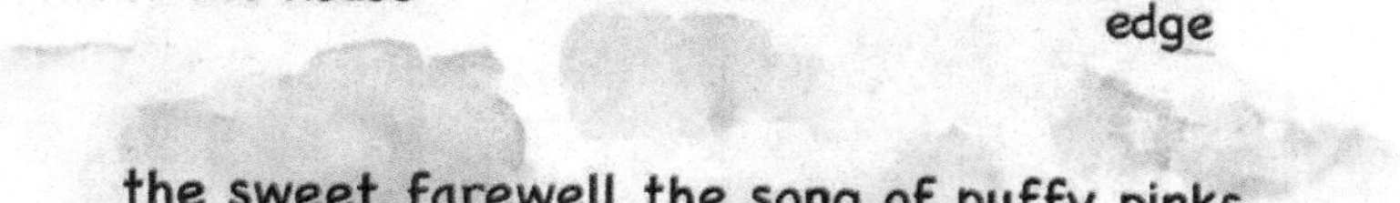

the sweet farewell the song of puffy pinks
and babyblues seen at dusk in the distance

Now
the night
swallows
up the sun
   AGAIN
over and over

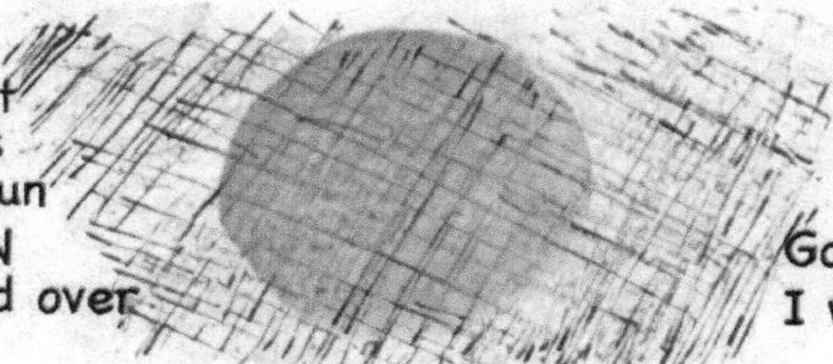

Good-bye
I whisper

Wishing my husband
could be like the sun

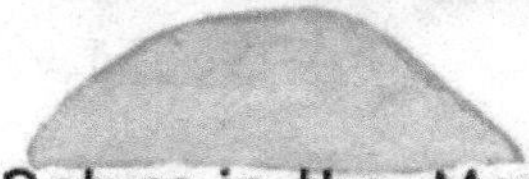

And Return in the Morning

Everything • Everything

Changed

Instantly, I was a widow.

I put on the red scarf Mitch
had given me.

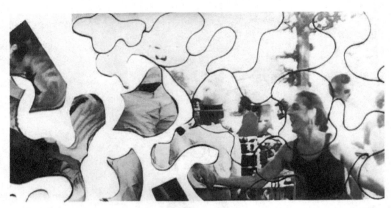

# WHY IS IT SO HARD TO BE A WIDOW?

WE WERE A UNIT
LIKE A PUZZLE ALL
OUR PIECES
FIT TOGETHER

IMAGINE ONE
DAY half the
PIECES GONE

WHAT DO
YOU DO WITH
THE LEFT OVER
PIECES?

KEEP THEM
IN A BOX?
RENDER THE
WHOLE PUZZLE
USELESS?

TRY TO FIND
THE LOST
PIECES?

I AM THE
LEFT OVER
PIECES OF
THAT PUZZLE

TRYING
SO HARD
TO FIND
A NEW

BOX TO
FIT THE
OLD PIECES
IN

NEW
BOX

# Chapter 2
# The Funeral

*When a person is born, we rejoice.*
*And when they're married, we jubilate.*
*But when they die, we try to pretend*
*nothing happened.*

Margaret Mead

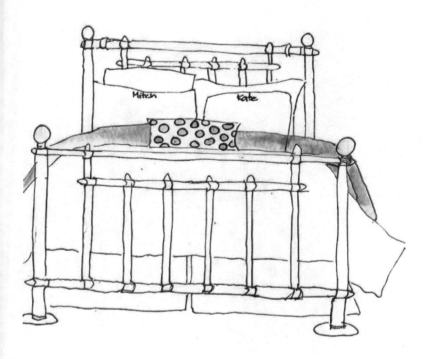

**M**itch and I slept in an old, brass, double bed that we inherited from his grandparents. That first night, after he died, I couldn't sleep alone so my oldest, dear friend Sheila stayed with me. Together we moved the bed to the other side of the room. My side of the bed was open, not against a wal.l But Mitch's side where Sheila slept was under the eaves. So, every time Sheila got out of bed, she'd hit her head and look over

at me. Several times we laughed, several times we didn't. I stil
only sleep on my side of the bed.

We followed Jewish tradition
and buried Mitch in 24 hours.
We held the funeral at our City Hall.
He would have been happy; he got a big crowd.

I was sitting in the front row
wrapped in the arms of my children.
I didn't see our friends and family
or hear the speeches. I was just waiting for
Mitch to return to his seat, and like he always did,
put his arm around me.

We buried Mitch on October 17, 2010.

We sat Shivah
at my house for three days.

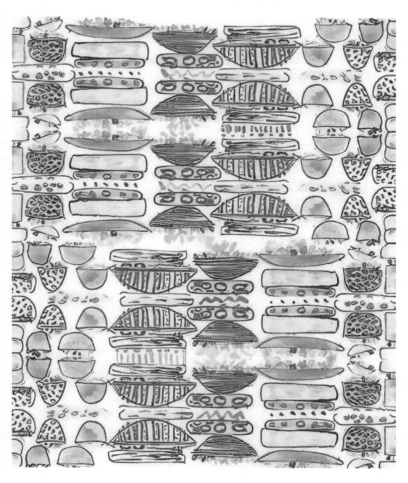

People brought beautiful food.
My refrigerator was overstuffed, leaving two
broken bins for me to live with.

# Chapter 3
# Widowing Together

*Widow Brain is a term used to describe the fogginess and disconnect that can set in after the death of a spouse.*

When I got married in 1977, I didn't think of anything negative, like who would die first (although I knew someone had to). I was thinking "forever." I was in love with only positive thoughts. I never imagined an ending to our life together. I never wanted to see the end.

I was not a stranger to death and the lives of widows. Both my mother and my dear Aunt Mary were widows. My mother at age 45 was left with five children and no life insurance and my aunt at age 36 was left with three children and a nursing career. I never imagined I would be like them. But now, many years into widowhood, I have joined them and the other 11.8 million widows in America.

Being a widow is a singular kind of displacement, entirely different from any other kind of separation. Sometimes couples who were your best friends when your husband was alive are no longer as interested.

Every day in the United States, approximately 2,800 women become widows. We are a very large demographic.

# Who are these widows?

They are our:
mothers,
sisters,
aunts,
cousins,
friends, and
ourselves.

What happens to the woman who
lost her loved one?

Instantly she becomes a single woman —

a widow.

It hurts to be a widow.

Like a punch in the gut or a
hard slap in the face.

When my husband died, I was in a
widow fog, numb, in a state of shock.

I was now part of a new widow world. A club I
never wanted to belong to. Being a widow is
not a choice, it just happens to you.

Almost half the women over 65 in the US are
widows, seven in ten live alone.

A widow's job is to grieve and mourn. It takes as long as she needs.

**Grieving is the inner pain, while mourning is the outer world of funerals and other rituals.**

After many years of being in a deep relationship, you fuse together. Even though you have your own independent core, his needs become yours and yours his. Your arm gets folded into the sleeve of his coat. His legs help you to walk faster. His smile defines joy, his laugh becomes happiness. Without realizing it, you are entwined and enmeshed.

Then he dies…

For a time, you continue to be entwined.

Slowly, he begins to wither away, and you start the long, hard process of untangling from him.

The untangling, the separating, the deconstructing—is grieving.

It takes as long as the widow needs.

The job of the new widow is to find all her own parts and put them together again in a new way and create a new life.

It takes as long as it takes.

## Chapter 4
# Widow Finances

*"The death of a spouse is one of the most devastating events of a person's life. To make matters worse, at a time when you feel incapable of dealing with life's routines, you're slammed with an avalanche of financial tasks that require immediate attention. This can be particularly stressful if the surviving spouse, usually the wife, did not play an active role in the household finances."*

Susan B. Garland
*A To-Do List for the Surviving Spouse.*

After the funeral and sitting shivah, my children started figuring out how they could help me. I guess they were a little nervous leaving me with the finances. Mitch had always taken care of our money and now I would have to navigate all our financial and legal paperwork by myself.

Immediately, I had to pay the bill to the funeral home for $9,100.00. Luckily, I could cover the check because I had just received the life Insurance money.

The kids gathered a team of friends and family; a lawyer, a banker, a dear friend, themselves, and one of my brothers to help me, teach me, and love me.

For two weeks my dining room table became the center of activity. Some bills were put on automatic pay while others were just put on a list. A new accountant was hired. I met with him, he was warm and welcoming. He had a financial planner who worked with him and so I worked with her.

My new lawyer explained that we had to go to probate court and transfer my car and building into my name. They had been in Mitch's name only. It was strange to discover my car really wasn't mine yet.

Everyone on my team was very supportive. But really, I was terrified and overwhelmed.

Was I capable of taking care of myself?

My children?

My car?

My house?

My yard?

My plumbing?

And then I thought, *Who will take out the garbage?*

I felt alone and afraid. I felt that way because I was alone and afraid. Mitch was gone.

Before I knew it, two weeks had gone by, and the children had to return to their lives. It was difficult to let them go.

Many widows lose their incomes when their husbands die, but because Mitch and I bought "the building" from his father, I have had a good enough income all these years. Owning a big building requires a lot of work but I have enjoyed being a "good" landlord. Caring about the lives of my tenants and being understanding when the rent was late.

I wish I could tell you that I am just fine now and that I've learned all the financial tasks, but honestly, I never got the hang of most of it. Finally, now years later, I hired a bookkeeper who works directly with my accountant. I worship them both.

*More to say…*

## A Financial Confession:
## Money, Fear, and Anxiety

Ten years later I find I am still feeling "Widow Finance Dread." I don't know if that's a real condition or if I just made it up, but I have it. Often, I feel like I'm falling off a cliff when I think of my finances. I pay my bills, cry, and feel fear. The lucky part is that I can pay my bills.

I never know in my bones if I am a rich widow or a poor widow. I go out to dinner with the confidence of a rich widow, and when the check arrives, I feel a little flutter of anxiety. Can I afford this dinner out for $33.14 tip and tax included, or the dinner for the whole family to celebrate an event? I am the matriarch; I feel the need to protect my children and do what Mitch would have done: pay for everyone. Now the children are older, more settled. They don't need me to pay for family dinners out anymore. That's a relief. Mostly they pick up the tab now.

For me, money and loss are linked together. Sometimes I think I'm feeling anxiety about money, but really, I'm sad and lonely.

Those feelings get morphed into worrying about the bills. I think the reason they are linked is because when Mitch died, I was financially dependent on him, so losing him also meant losing my security, both emotional and financial. I think perhaps for many widows these feelings are temporary, but for me, I am triggered by the original loss of my father who died while I was in my second year of college. My mother was only 45 years old, left with five children and no money. My father was only 47. He did not leave a life insurance policy (like Mitch did for me) or any savings. Now, so many years after both my parents' deaths, I think I am still carrying my mother's fear about money. I never realized my fear was really hers and belonged to her, not me.

Hopefully that means I can now give it up and get past crying when I pay my phone bill.

*p.s. I have been paying the kids (Sasha and Noah's) phone bill all these years. Now they want to pay mine. What a gift!*

# Chapter 5
# His Things

would like to introduce you to Mitch through some of his iconic possessions.

Mitch's therapy chair.

## Mitch's T-shirt

**long sleeve black tee**

Before I became a widow, I just wore black and grey. Occasionally I would wear a black and grey patterned top. Now all I want to wear is an old, black, long-sleeved T-shirt of Mitch's. I was so happy when I found it folded in his draw unwashed, with just the hint of his smell still lingering.

Immediately, I put it on and would find myself wearing it to bed every night. And on days when I worked at home, I'd just leave it on all day.

## Sperry Boating Shoes

Mitch found Sperry's when he started sailing with his friends in high school. The shoes fit his wide, flat foot perfectly. When he died, there were seven pairs left in his closet. Because he had seven pairs of the same shoes, he needed to remember which pair went together, which ones were older, newer. He couldn't tell by looking, so he numbered them "#1" being the oldest, the ones he wore when he was working in the garden or painting the house, and "#7," the newest, the ones he'd wear out to a nice dinner. I bring up the shoes because I couldn't bear to throw them out, so I created shoe-flower-centerpieces for our Thanksgiving table. I put some beautiful flowers and herbs in just-enough dirt, so they would last the weekend.

Kate Seidman

## The Old LL Bean Jacket in My Closet
*This illustration was painted by my dear friend,*
*Loren Doucette.*

This morning I walked by the half-open front hall closet. As I look inside, my eyes immediately focus on a classic L.L. Bean jean jacket Mitch wore to work and everywhere, every day, for the last 15 years of his life. I notice it still holds his shape.

One rogue arm suggests he is reaching for me, he is asking me to dance. I can almost hear Ella and Louie singing "I won't dance don't ask me, I won't dance how could I…" In my mind, I am doing the Lindy with Mitch the way we always did, smooth and easy, with style.

Now the memories of Mitch and the many moments we shared are flooding my mind…

"Breathe, relax your arm.

Breathe, relax your face.

Breathe, breathe, breathe…"

In six short hours, our first child, Aaron Murray Seidman Cohen, came out of me and into the world. Mitch was my coach, and I was an Amazon woman—the strongest, bravest, the most powerful woman in the Universe.

More memories are coming; swimming naked in the early morning before anyone is awake at Duck pond on our yearly week vacation in Wellfleet. Going to Vietnam with our middle child Noah while he was in the Peace Corps in the Philippines. Walking on Good Harbor Beach for 30-plus years. Kissing madly on the backshore the first time I came to visit Mitch's family, Gloucester 1977.

He taught me the true meaning of *tikkun olam*, repairing the world. Mitch repaired all broken things, both human and man-made. He could fix anything: a light switch, a plug, stereo equipment, his car, my car, and the people who came to him for therapy.

I am there with him, feeling him there with me, knowing he is not and never will be with me in real time again.

## The Van

The Plymouth Voyager

Mitch was a practical person. He never liked to throw anything away if it was still working, his junky old van was no exception.

When Mitch died, Aaron was 31, Noah was 27, and Sasha 22. Noah won the van in a game of rock-paper-scissors with Sasha.

My instincts, my hope was, that by opening three bank accounts, my kids would feel protected. But no one is protected when the guy who is the rock of the family dies suddenly. So, we huddled together in the van and became the family support group

"The Family Bubble"

59

## Chapter 6
# Holidays—The First Year After Mitch's Death

*The life of the dead is placed
in the heart of the living.*

Cicero

On October 24th, only ten days after Mitch died, I turned 63. My friends created a ritual birthday celebration for me. Each of them contributing a square of fabric that reminded them of me or that they thought I would like. The squares were sewn together and made into a shawl. The predominant colors turned out to be a silvery grey. It was beautiful, perfect for my hair that was also turning silvery grey.

The concept was that I would be bathed in friendship, protected, and loved. It worked. And to this day when I put on my shawl, I feel their love. I am reminded of their kindness and generosity, and I am aware of how much healing I have done.

## One Month Later—Thanksgiving Weekend
## Shopping at HomeGoods Before Thanksgiving

For 30 years, Mitch and I hosted Thanksgiving for both our families, which included his two sisters, three out of my four brothers, plus all the nieces and nephews. Each family brought a favorite dish or two. And everyone brought wine. My sister-in-law Ana brought her amazing chestnut/sausage stuffing that became a favorite. Ana was horrified every year when I wanted to cook our bird unstuffed. I thought stuffing the bird dried it out while Ana believed her stuffing gave flavor and moistness to the entire event. Finally, after many years, we solved the bird-stuffing problem by making two turkeys—one dressed, one undressed. Compromise works.

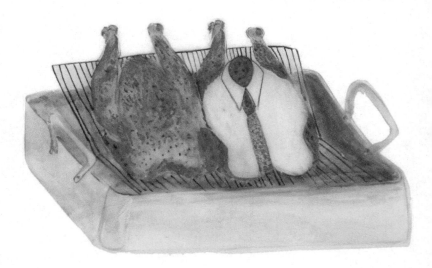

I learned how to make a turkey (breast down, 15 minutes a pound, undressed) from my mother-in-law. She was a gourmet cook who watched Julia Child on TV and learned French cooking. She was a force and helped create the first women's consciousness-raising group on Cape Ann in 1970. A few years later, she went back to school and became a sex therapist. She was always very kind to me and grateful that I gave her a grandchild and brought her only son back to live near her.

```
Foom the kitchen of: Sylvia Cohen
Recipe for: Kate -Thanksgiving Turkey
Ingredients: 2 Turkeys take more time
Turkey
Salt/pepper/ peprika    [1 Tbsp. salt
orange                  [1 Tesp. pepper
                        [1 Tesp. paprika
350° oven - 15 minutes a lb.
Wash and dry bird
Put spice mixture in cavity -
Cut orange and put in cavity
put spice mixture all over bird
```

Cook breast down. Last 20 minutes turn over
and roast until golden brown.

It was the Monday before Thanksgiving. I was meeting Aaron and (his wife) Katie for dinner. I was a little early and decided to stop at HomeGoods. I love making our Thanksgiving table look elegant. I needed extra coffee cups and potholders. I didn't know what else I needed, but I would walk the aisles and see what struck me as necessities. This was not a new ritual; I would do this visit to HomeGoods before every Thanksgiving and when I would return home, Mitch was there to ask me, "Do we really need a new carving knife or a new cutting board or a new anything?" I would feel bad, like a child who had done something wrong, but I would tell Mitch that whatever purchase I had just made was essential to the success of our Thanksgiving meal. Eventually I wore him down. He even started saying, "Kate, you should have whatever you want. We've both worked hard enough all these years, I'm not going to worry about a few bucks one way or another."

As I was walking the aisles of HomeGoods, I started to have this discussion with Mitch. It was just there in my head, about what I was buying, and did we really need it? It took me by surprise. Mitch wouldn't be home to ask me the question, *Did I need the coffee cups I was about to buy for $14.95?*

My heart began to hurt. *Oh my God, Mitch isn't going to be here for the first time since we started this family ritual in 1980, the year after Aaron was born.*

How was it possible?

# The Weekend

I don't know how Sasha managed to miss her plane and still get home earlier than originally expected, but that's Sasha.

It was the Tuesday before Thanksgiving. Sasha was the first of my children to arrive. Her plane landed at 10:20 p.m. and I picked her up at the airport. For the next two days, relatives started arriving. Aaron, Katie, and Noah plus two of my brothers came on Wednesday night for a pre-Thanksgiving meal. Everyone else came on Thursday before 4 p.m. when dinner was served. The relatives gathered. There are 23 of us seated around the dining room table. It's the first time since the funeral that we are all together. It feels so normal and yet I am not at all normal.

I welcome everyone and say a few awkward words about the centerpieces I made out of Mitch's old Sperrys filled with tiny purple daisies. I think it's funny and pretty creative to have found such a novel use for these, now otherwise, useless objects.

It never occurred to me that anyone would be offended by putting shoes on the table. Years later, I found out that my brother-in-law was horrified, but he couldn't say anything and insult "the widow hostess."

We do buffet style. We have placed all the food on the built-in, half-round pine kitchen island Mitch built. We're all helping ourselves to whatever food we desire. Mitch has made so many beautiful things in our house that we all feel his presence. It is very difficult for everyone, but especially for his dad, who eats a small amount of food and wants to leave. He is weak, getting frail, although he is still healthy. He misses his son. We all do.

I am attempting to confront the elephant in the room. We all know we have just experienced a huge loss, so I think it's better to say something.

I encourage everyone to share Mitch stories. "Just tap your wine glass with your spoon, get everyone's attention whenever you're ready."

No one speaks.

As we eat our Thanksgiving meal, my brothers share with me that they want to visit me every other weekend for the next year. I am very pleased and grateful for their love.

Finally, a spoon hits a glass. My brother Dan breaks the silence. He has a Mitch story. Soon others follow. They have Mitch stories. Finally, we are all talking about Mitch. I am happy. I miss him.

Over this long weekend, I realize how much Mitch made things happen. And how dependent I was on him and his amazing ability to know definitively what to do and how to do it, what to say and how to say it. Now I am just beginning to understand that I will have to make things happen for myself.

## Chapter 7

# Learning to Grieve

*"Grief, I've learned, is just love. It's all the love you want to give but cannot. All of that unspent love gathers up in the corners of your eyes, the lump in your throat, and in that hollow part of your chest. Grief is just love with no place to go."*

Anonymous

Today people are encouraged to grieve the death of their loved ones and to experience the pain for as long as needed. That was not the case in 1968 when my father, who was 47 years old, died from heart complications. In those days, people didn't want to look at death. Instead, they tried to deny it. Consequently, I never learned how to grieve his death. When I became a widow, I had much to learn about how to grieve for my husband.

# Was I doing "Widow" correctly?

I felt self-conscious, were people talking about me?

in my head the gossip sounded like this:

" She's too well dressed to be a widow."

" You know she's still going to Stop & Shop and buying food."

" I heard she doesn't cry very much — maybe she never loved Mitch."

I felt like a kid in grade school!

I decided to give myself a report card.

How was I doing as a widow?

## Widow Report Card

2010 - 2018 marking period
For: Katherine Susan Seidman
Given by: self

| | 1st | 2nd | 3rd | 4th |
|---|---|---|---|---|
| **Finance** | | | | |
| Looking at Bank Statements | F | | | |
| Following the money | D⁻ | | | |
| Giving money away | A | | | |
| **Grieving** | | | | |
| Crying and Sobbing | D | | | |
| Moving on | D | | | |
| Emotions | C | | | |
| **Funeral** | | | | |
| Place | A | | | |
| Speakers | A | | | |

| | 1st | 2nd | 3rd | 4th |
|---|---|---|---|---|
| **Holidays** | | | | |
| Thanksgiving | A | | | |
| Christmas/Channukah | C⁻ | | | |
| Yom Kippur | B⁺ | | | |
| 1st Birthday | B | | | |
| **Moving on with life** | | | | |
| on the surface | B⁺ | | | |
| under the surface | D⁻ | | | |
| Adventures | B⁺ | | | |
| Travel | A⁻ | | | |
| Dating | C⁻ | | | |
| Dancing | A⁺ | | | |

I was in a widow fog for a few years. During one visit to my doctor, I said I was feeling sad about Mitch. Immediately he suggested I take anti-depressants. What? Why did he want to keep me away from my pain? I wanted to feel it, not suppress it. And I wanted help dealing with all the overwhelming feelings I was having.

Mitch had been a therapist. We saw individual therapists and couple therapists throughout our marriage, so I felt very comfortable asking a few friends for a referral.

I started seeing a wonderful therapist who I quickly trusted. He was warm and kind and smart. Weekly I was crying, sighing, and moaning. I realized how loved I was and how much I loved and lost. I was facing my grief and understanding how deep it went.

# Grief Revealed

Grief is water

Moving

Flowing

It comes in waves

Unpredictable

Squeezes through

And seeps into your spirit

Grief is a river

meandering along

switching back and forth

sculpting new patterns

into the landscape of your life.

Grief doesn't stop until it becomes part of you

Grief grabs hold like a tick in summer

Grief gets under your skin and

sucks your blood

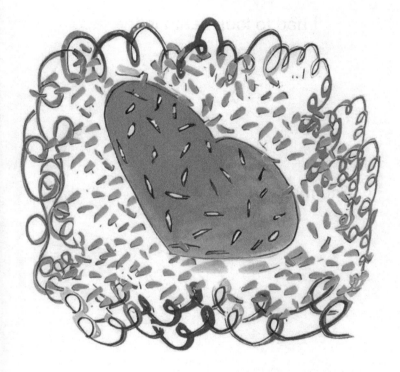

Grief attacks the heart

Leaving broken shards of love

Scattered

Grief crawled into my life unnoticed

When I was most vulnerable

When my only, favorite husband died

I had to look death in the face

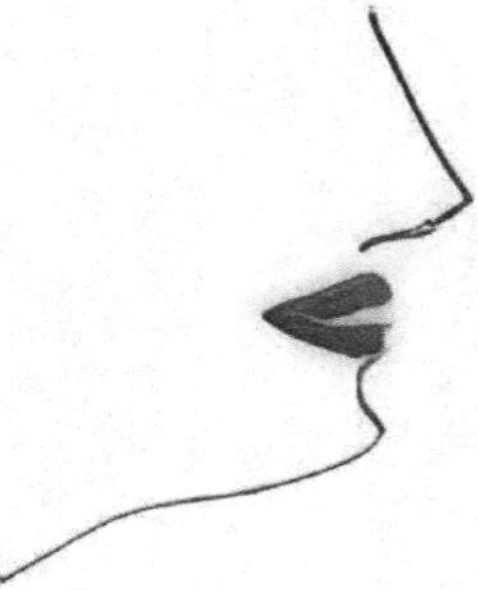

And make friends with it

Or my heart would surely break

And never be repaired.

How do you mend a
broken heart?

Sew it together
with heavy thread

Soak it in Epsom salt

Sing to it

Find another

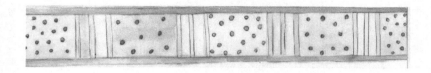

## Chapter 8
# Widow Health—Eczema or Psoriasis?

*A range of studies reveal the powerful effects grief can have on the body. Grief increases inflammation, which can worsen health problems you already have and cause new ones.*

*Web*MD, July 2019

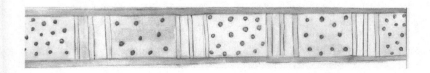

couldn't cry and sob like you see in the movies. I was able to get a few scrawny tears out but nothing robust, nothing I could be proud of. I wanted to sob so badly, I wanted to be able to express the excruciating pain I was feeling. Let out all the sadness within me. But I was filled with fear. I had always cried with Mitch, with him I felt safe. Now, without him, I just wasn't safe. So, all that pent up emotion had to go somewhere—it came out of my heart and moved into my skin. I have come to understand that unconsciously one of the ways I express my grief is through my skin. The skin is the largest organ in our body. I never had serous skin problems as a child, young adult, or even as a middle-aged person. But after Mitch died, my skin slowly began erupting.

It started in my mouth with my gums. They turned bright red and bled when I brushed my teeth.

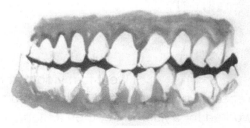

My dentist said, "Kate, this is not surprising. You're a new widow and your gums are showing your stress level."

I didn't know then that widows have more stress than other people or that my stress could manifest throughout my body as an itchy belly, cracked hands, and flaking feet. This didn't happen all at once. In fact, it took many years.

My gums soon healed, but one day I noticed that my belly was itchy. I saw a rash. It was red, a little raw and evenly spaced on either side of my belly button. I thought it odd to have a rash so evenly spaced.

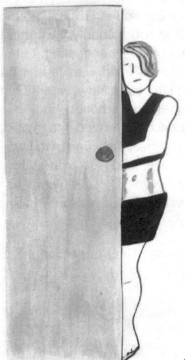

I went to my doctor. He thought it might be eczema and suggested a simple topical cream. I used it. It worked for a little while, then it stopped working. I started collecting all kinds of creams that were recommended by both professionals and friends.

Now I have an amazing collection of every kind of skin cream.

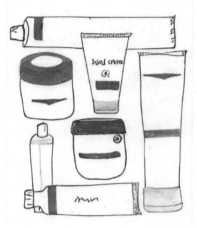

One very snowy and cold winter, my hands looked terrible, like I had cut them. Again, I thought this was my unexpressed grief. Then, as spring arrived, the cuts magically disappeared. My hands were healing. I was grateful.

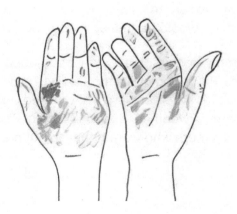

Several months later, I got out of bed and now my feet were cracked and flakey.

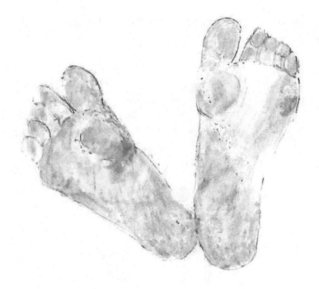

My disease had moved again deep into the last place the grief could escape from: my feet. Was this my grief's journey through my body?

Several doctors diagnosed me with eczema while others told me it was definitely psoriasis. The last doctor I went to told me to mix two creams together, rub them on the bottom of my feet, and I would be healed in four weeks.

I lost faith in my doctors. I knew my body needed to be in a warm place. I no longer wanted to live in New England during the winter. My feet were still cracked and itchy. I felt better in warmer weather. I took a trip to Florida. I have several friends there who were happy to put me up for a few days.

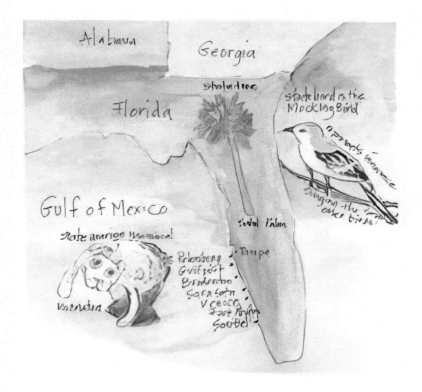

I fell in love with one of the towns I visited during that trip.

Several years later, I am still plagued with itchy, flakey feet. I went to a healer in Florida, recommended by a friend. I lay down on her quartz healing table and drank the green tea she suggested I drink. Even green tea didn't heal me.

# Chapter 9
# Gravestone—Forever Loved

*"Grief is not a disorder, a disease, or a sign of weakness. It is an emotional, physical, and spiritual necessity. The price you pay for love. The only cure for grief is to grieve."*

Earl Grollman,
author of *Living When a Loved One Has Died*

In the Jewish tradition, within the first year after a loved one's death, the family and other mourners gather at the gravesite for the "unveiling ceremony:" the placing of the tombstone. The grave marker is put in place and the monument is formally dedicated.

I got a call from the cemetery committee at the temple. They wanted me to decide what to write on Mitch's tombstone. It was time for his unveiling. At first the task felt overwhelming. Whatever I wrote would be written in stone. What could I say that would be meaningful enough for all eternity?

One day I was going through old letters and birthday poems from Mitch. I found a poem written for my 60th birthday. Mitch wrote that he would love me through all eternity. When he wrote it and I originally read it I didn't notice the thought *through all eternity*. I just took it for granted, didn't focus on how special it was. But now it had more meaning. Now I think what good fortune to have found this message from Mitch. I will never lose him. We will be together through all time. It's a lot of pressure to write in stone, but I knew what I wanted to say—*Forever Loved*—that I will love him forever.

The stone I picked for Mitch is like no other in the Jewish cemetery. It is a sculpture cut out of Cape Ann granite. Family and friends and old clients come to visit him there.

It is a tradition to leave a small stone to show that they visited.

Mitch is on the right side, my place on the left, is waiting for me. We will be forever nestled together in this little cemetery in West Gloucester.

# Part Two

# *Beyond Grief*

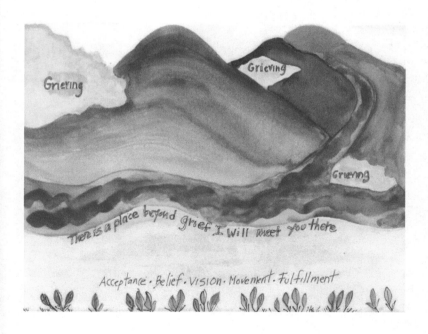

## Chapter 10
# New Ways to Think
# Messages from Mitch

*Look up at the stars and not down at your feet. Try to make sense of what you see and wonder about what makes the Universe exist. Be curious.*

Stephen Hawking

The day after Mitch died, the world felt different to me. I thought, *Is there something happening here that I never noticed before?* Perhaps something divine, a kind of magic working in the Universe I had never believed before? I wanted magic and I was open to anything that could connect me to Mitch.

My prayers are with you as you mourn his passing on the physical plane and adapt to life with him in Spirit.

This note from an artist acquaintance woke me up. *Is it true?* Mitch is dead but not gone, only missing on the physical plane. What did she mean—*spirit?* He was in my heart and in my thoughts every day. I had to open my eyes and keep them open. Weirdly, the world seemed brighter. I was more aware of the beauty all around me. The flowers, the birds, the ocean, the colors. I could no longer take anything for granted. I was becoming myself.

When I look at the digital clock in my car, the number 24 is often staring back at me: 5:24; 8:24; 10:24. When I first noticed this number thing, I tried to make sense of it. It felt like every time I looked at a clock, I saw a 24, which is my lucky number.

Then I'd notice 10/24 (my birth date). I started talking out loud to Mitch about it. Quickly I got that he was communicating with me, just saying *hi* or sending me a kiss. The 10:24 (my birthday) was a more serious conversation he wanted to have. He wanted me to notice, be conscious, and pay attention. When people talk about a sign, is this it? Is there such a thing as a sign?

During his second year of law school, Noah had an internship in Camden, New Jersey. On his first day, he was a little nervous. He arrived at the courthouse, carefully walked up the front steps, looked up, and was shocked to see his father's name etched into the granite façade: Mitchell H. Cohen.

Immediately, he took a picture and sent it to me. What an amazing coincidence. Noah and I believe his dad was with him as he entered the courthouse that morning. We never did find out what the "H." was for. Mitch's middle initial is S.

In October of 2012, I took a writing and bookmaking class at Penland Craft School near Ashland, North Carolina. When I told the kids I was taking this class, they were delighted. Sasha immediately suggested I drive instead of fly, saying the scenery was magnificent in the Blue Ridge Mountains. It was fall. The trees would be turning into a million shades of red, orange, and gold, a visual event I did not want to miss. I thought, *What a good idea*. I said yes. I got in my

Prius, trusting in the Universe, heading toward the unknown. From Gloucester to Penland was a fourteen-hour drive. I made a few stops visiting friends and family along the way. Then I got to the foot of the mountain and began the steep climb upward.

Before I knew it, I was in several inches of snow with no cell phone service. When I travel, I use my GPS in my phone to guide me to my destination. However, that was no longer possible. So, I just kept driving. Up, up the mountain.

Where was I?

I was beginning to worry. Then out of nowhere a huge sign appeared.

Mitch was guiding me. I had a sign (literally) I was okay. I arrived exhausted, with a cold, but happy to be at my destination.

## April 2013
## Once Again Dancing Came Into My Life

Laurie, an acquaintance, had stage 4 lung cancer. She had limited time left on the planet and spent as much time dancing as she could. Dancing made her happy and content. Every Friday night she went to a dance at the Armenian Center in Watertown, Massachusetts. She invited me along with several other single women she cared about to join her. She believed dancing could cure her cancer and my broken heart.

The first time I went with Laurie to "the dance," there were five of us. At the door we each paid $15 and walked into an old school gym. I looked around the gym and saw many older men and women learning a dance called the Lindy

Hop, a dance I learned in the third grade with my best friend Laura Rubenstein. Dick Clark on his show *American Bandstand* made the Lindy famous in the 1950s. Originally it came from Harlem, couples danced to 1920s hot jazz. The dance is a partner dance: men and women meet each other, hold each other, and together do the steps they've learned seamlessly. Today we call it "Swing."

I had a great dance with a man who showed me the balboa, a dance I had never heard of before. A dance invented by people who had small dance halls. They did all the same moves as the Lindy-Hoppers, only they did it close and small. He held me, led me—one, two, three, hold—one, two, three, hold. It was a new variation and so much fun. He could lead and I could follow. When the song ended, I started to return to where my group of friends were sitting, resting a little, in-between songs. I looked around the room looking for my next partner. Then I saw a clump of gorgeous curly silver and black hair across the room. I watched him as he waited patiently for someone to ask him to dance. A woman went over to him, instantly they gracefully moved smoothly around the dance floor. Mesmerized, I stood there watching him until the song ended. By the time the next song started, I was dancing with him.

His movements were so familiar, like we had danced together for years. I asked him his name and when he told me his name was Paul (not Mitch), I was surprised. Soon the song was over. It's not proper etiquette at the dance to keep dancing with the same partner, so I moved away and almost fell as I sat back into my chair.

I whispered to Laurie, "See that guy across the room with the curly hair? Who does he look like?" She looked and knew immediately. He looked like Mitch. I decided to be normal about this very abnormal experience. I continued dancing with so many others—a Steve, a Marty, a guy named Web. All of these men were very good dancers. It was so much fun. Laurie kept telling them all what a good dancer I was, so they kept asking me to dance. It was a great feeling to be appreciated by these dancing men.

Then he appeared before me, standing as he had when I first saw him, swaying to the music waiting for someone to ask him to dance. He had moved from across the dance floor to right in front of me. Was he there waiting for me to ask him to dance? I waited as he danced with several women. I watched in disbelief at how much he danced like Mitch. I was drawn to him like a magnet. Powerless, I got up and walked toward him. He seemed to know I was ready to dance and so we danced again.

Paul and I always danced together whenever we were at the same venue. One afternoon, my cousin June and her daughter, who is also named Sasha, came to Boston to look at colleges. We met for lunch and took a walk on the greenway. There was a stage set up, swing music playing, and a group dancing on the makeshift dance floor. Immediately I wished for Paul to appear and have a quick dance. Just as I had this thought, I felt a tap on my shoulder. Yes, it was Paul. We had a divine dance and then each went our separate ways.

# Chapter 11
# Widow Dating

*I know you're gone you're not coming back.*
*I'm letting go I'm ready to live with that.*
*Dear George, our love is everlasting.*
*It's you're blessing I am asking for.*
*As I open my heart to another, companion,*
*friend, and lover, someone who isn't you.*

"Dear George," used with permission from
Sloan Wainwright, singer/songwriter

I've been seeing a very nice man. Yesterday my ankles started itching. I thought: oh dear, my eczema has returned then I saw some red blotches on my elbow—then hives came out on my face.

I can't tell if the reason I broke out in hives is because I like him or because I don't like him.

Widow talking to herself about dating

A) guilt:
I know Mitch has been
dead for 7 years if I
date will he be jealous?

B) Bad logic:
Maybe he'll come back
and I'll be unavailable.

c) Worse than bad logic:
He'll be so angry he'll
never speak to me again.

After Mitch's death, I continued working, both teaching art at a school for troubled teens and selling awesome women's clothing at my shop, The Art Room. The shop was a natural place for friends and strangers to gather, find a gift, talk to me, and hang out for hours. It was perfect for me at that early time of widowhood. People knew they were always welcome, and I didn't have to ask for companionship. I didn't have to call anyone, they just magically appeared.

Two months before my 65th birthday, I was answering emails when up popped *Senior People Meet*, an online dating service. I laughed and thought, *How unsexy—for old people?* I thought I'd check it out. I joined. I have always been comfortable around men as I had four great brothers and a father who loved me dearly. Even though it had only been less than two years since I was widowed, I thought I would see what online dating was like.

I went into the site and looked around. How innocent I was, not knowing how addictive and time-consuming it would be. I had to provide a profile picture and a written description of myself. I also needed to describe the person I was hoping to meet, which meant I needed to know who I was and what I wanted. I felt overwhelmed. I had no idea who I was anymore, and I had even less of an idea who I wanted to meet.

For a while, every time I spoke to any of my friends who were savvy "online daters," I'd grill them for information. Each of them had their own ideas of what was the best way to fill out the empty spaces on the form—be funny, be cute, be brief, be serious, be yourself. I filled out my profile trying to be all those things.

But most important of all, I had a great picture of myself.

Once in the site, I was amazed. I'd go in, and before I knew it, hours had passed. Online I could "shop" for men, easily seeing 50 at a clip.

I'm a great shopper; I enjoy the process. In general, one needs to enjoy shopping to find someone special in the overwhelming line up of criminal-looking headshots of men. Even I would start to get nauseous and cranky after seeing too many overweight, bald, bearded, white-haired old white men with their lecherous arms around their young, beautiful daughters. I had filled out the forms, put in my great picture, but no one was interested in my profile—I didn't get any flirts or emails. What was I doing wrong?

A week later, my brother Dan came to visit. I mentioned I was having trouble with online dating. Sweetly, he offered to go on with me. After reading my profile, he made a few quick, easy-to-change suggestions. We began a search, and he noticed a man who "cared about the world of ideas." We looked at his pictures. He didn't look like a killer. He was kind of handsome, standing in a yellow cashmere sweater in front of a painted portrait of a woman; another with his graduating yoga class surrounded by eight good-looking young women. He was square jawed, and I guessed he was Scandinavian from his name and appearance. I decided to make him my first "online man." I wrote him an email asking what his ideas were and telling him that I lived in Gloucester.

Good Harbor Beach

Off it went into cyber space. Then—amazingly—he wrote back! Maybe on-line dating did work, maybe there really were men out there wanting to meet me. He knew Gloucester and asked me what it was like to live there. I took my time and wrote from my heart about my feelings for Gloucester. I immediately got a response. We started a correspondence—like in the old days—writing and waiting for a letter, the difference being our letters took only moments to send and receive. We continued writing for a few days until he asked if he could call me.

I was about to go on the trip to Penland Craft School. We spent the next two weeks being in touch, texting and talking for hours on the phone—like I did when I was a teenager. I began to feel like a teenager, he was so easy to talk to. I liked him.

From our frequent conversations, I learned that his father was 28 years older than his mother. That his father, like my grandfather, fought in the Russian Revolution. His father's family was of Jewish decent, not Scandinavian. He was a child of a third marriage. His dad was famous and died when Tom was only nine. After his dad's death, his mother, who was having an affair with a woman, sent him off to boarding school. I knew a lot about him, but I didn't know him in the flesh, how sensitive and vulnerable he was. And he didn't know how much I loved Mitch.

"Hi, it's me, Tom. I'm returning a day early, I can't wait to meet you, let's meet on Saturday the 10th instead, okay?"

*Oh, really?* I responded reluctantly, "I guess that would work, except I'm working at the shop until 5:30."

"I'll just come to the shop when you're done, I'll bring a bottle of good wine that I got out in California. It'll be great."

I agreed, but deep inside I knew it was a bad idea. 11/11 @ 11 was such a perfect, romantic day, a perfect time to meet. 11/10/12 was incorrect, not in sequence.

Tom arrived at the shop just as I was closing. The last customer had bought a beautiful dress for her daughter's wedding. It was elegant and so was the mother of the bride. As Tom walked through the door, I immediately noticed his handsome face and sweet smile. He looked just like his on-line photos. Although we had talked on the phone many times, meeting for the first time made us both feel a little nervous. He quickly sat down at the green round table in the window of my shop. Tom asked for two wine glasses and soon we were sipping the wine he had brought from California. Outside the sky was turning dark grey. As we finished our second glass of wine I suddenly, out of the blue, kissed him on his mouth. I was a little tipsy, and clearly, a little turned on. Tom was taken by surprise and immediately suggested we go to dinner and get out of the window where everyone walking by had full view of us. We went to dinner around the corner at The Franklin where I knew most of the patrons. Tom and I went to the bar and sat too close to each other. I was almost sitting in his lap, trying to be normal, but I just wasn't. We ordered. Salmon to share and another glass of red wine for each of us. A half hour later, Tom paid the bill and we were on the sidewalk in front of the restaurant. I wasn't ready to say goodnight. Innocently I blurted out, "Why don't you come back to my house?" I was naive and unsophisticated. Clearly, I didn't know the rules of online dating. Plus my house was still as it had been when I was married, pictures everywhere of my previous life.

He arrived at my house, sat down on the couch, looked up, saw a beautiful picture of Mitch and me, and said, "I like Mitch."

He saw the wall of photos of my family and said he had to leave. He wasn't prepared for the love he saw in those photos. The next and last time I saw him he explained to me that he couldn't see me anymore because he felt inadequate. He hadn't had a marriage like mine, and he felt he could never catch up, never be as important to me as Mitch was. And yes, we were doomed. After two dates I never saw him again. We were out of sequence. 11/10/12 was the wrong date to meet.

I was trying to find a new life with love in it. I was used to having love in my life and it was lonely not having a partner. Did I have to give Mitch up? Am I capable of grieving for Mitch and loving someone new at the same time?

I went on Match.com. I met a few men, dated, but no one was right. I was hoping to find someone who could understand the complexities of a mature relationship, perhaps someone who also had a long successful marriage.

I kept open and just kept saying YES…

(when it was possible).

Several years went by. My friend Ruth met a rabbi at a baby-naming. He was single and handsome. She asked him if he would like to meet her friend Kate. After they spoke, he said he was interested. Immediately Ruth texted: Kate would you like to meet a very nice rabbi?

*A rabbi?* I was surprised, neither Ruth nor I was religious, so I thought he must be a special rabbi for Ruth to like him enough to introduce us.

"Yes, sure, why not?" I replied ambivalently.

The next day, August 19th, I received a lovely email from Ruth's rabbi. He explained that he was interested in meeting me, but he was a very busy rabbi and would not be able to meet for several months as the high holidays were approaching and he had also promised to officiate at a wedding and perform a bris. He said he would understand if I were not interested.

I wrote back explaining that I too, was a very busy person. We would meet when the time was right. We started an email correspondence sharing our lives, past and present. He suggested we continue writing until we could meet in person. We'd find out if we had anything in common. It took almost four months for us to meet.

Again, Veteran's Day and the numbers 11/11 showed up. The Rabbi suggested we meet that day at the Beauport Hotel restaurant in Gloucester. I remembered I had wanted to meet my first on-line date on 11/11, but it didn't work out. I thought hopefully this time it would. I arrived at the hotel first. He was late. Later I learned he was usually late.

We spent five hours entranced and intoxicated—glued to each other. We had so much to talk about and the time went by so quickly. Finally, the waiter asked if we were finished with our meal, he needed our table. Would we mind leaving? We moved onto a couch in the lobby sitting as close to each other as possible. There was chemistry between us. Soon we were ready to leave the hotel. He walked me to my car and kissed me twice. I melted right there in the parking lot.

The Widow and The Rabbi

We continued emailing. I mentioned to him that I felt like Elizabeth Barrett Browning to his Robert, writing and receiving letters.

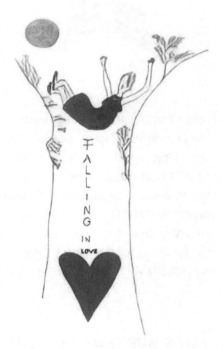

He sent me birthday flowers signing "Love, Robert." That was so romantic. I thought I was falling in love. By our third date, he only wanted to come to my house. I'd suggest: "I'll drive to your house, we could go out to dinner, hear music."

"No," he said, "I'd rather eat peanut butter with just you at your house than go out anywhere."

I didn't understand. It didn't feel like we were moving the relationship into a healthy, happy place. I wanted to expand, he wanted to contract.

At the time it didn't occur to me that he might have wanted to keep our new relationship a secret. He was a public person, a rabbi. Perhaps he was a womanizer? Was he keeping it secret? I had no idea. A few dates later he asked me why I chose to be a widow. *Chose to be a widow?* I was surprised. It was never a choice. It happened to me. But now it had been many years and I still thought of myself as a widow. Clearly, he thought it was a problem. Suddenly, the infatuation, the possibility of finding love again, was fading.

**Now, I was surrounded by red flags.**

The love, the heart, had flipped over and was now a sharp object ready to pierce me.

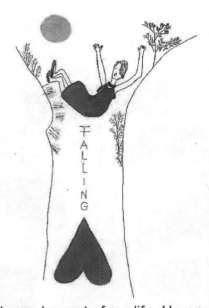

Mitch would always be part of my life. He would always be in my heart. I think I have room in there for Mitch and another as well. On our last date, again at my house, the rabbi kept talking about my involvement with being a widow. Why did I want to put on a widow's art show and keep writing on the subject? He said to me sadly, "We are just not compatible." Then he left. That was the end. I never saw him again. I was sorry to no longer have his wonderful kisses. This was the second time I met a man on Armistice Day—11/11—that I liked, and he liked me. But neither of them could accept that I had a husband who I will always love. I have room in my heart for another person, like in the song, "Dear George" by Sloan Wainwright, quoted in the beginning of this chapter. Please listen to the entire song online. I think it's great! My friend Nancy met Sloan while attending a music camp. When Nancy heard Sloan sing "Dear George," she immediately bought me the CD. I think Sloan has captured the widow dilemma so well. I listen to "Dear George" often and cry.

## Chapter 12
# Widow Travel

*Sometimes your only available transportation*
*is a leap of faith.*

Margaret Shepar

My life had a giant hole in it.

had traveled to Mexico, Italy, Vietnam, and the Philippines with Mitch. I knew from those trips that traveling was magical. I was hoping it could still be fulfilling now without him.

Mitch had left some money for me. I thought this was a good way to use it.

**I needed something wonderful in my life.**

# TRAVEL

I knew instinctively that if I went to a strange, new place for a limited amount of time, I would feel good about leaving the comfort of my home and hopefully discover what I was capable of. I needed to create a new normal and find out who I was becoming. Traveling afforded me time away from grieving. When I was traveling, I wasn't focusing on my loss, instead I was having new adventures.

When friends and family asked me to travel with them, I said, "YES!"

## Crete—March 2011

Only five months after Mitch died, a friend asked me to go to Crete with her and her husband. "Do you want to go to Crete? I have a cousin performing medieval music at a Jewish temple in Chania."

"Ah-um…oh…where is Crete?" I asked from my widow fog. "Okay, I'll go. Yes, okay."

"Oh, and Judy wants to come also."

"Sure, fine, okay. I like Judy."

After flying for ten hours, we arrived in Crete. We took a bus from the airport to Chania. As soon as we put our suitcases in our rooms, my friend and her husband wanted to go sightseeing. I, on the other hand, was exhausted and freezing. The wind was blowing hard on the Mediterranean. It was snowing in Athens. They thought it might snow in Chania. Luckily for me, it didn't.

I was in widow fog and could barely move. It was Judy who immediately saw how paralyzed I was and made it her business to stay close to me and make me her buddy for the entire trip. It turned out that the best part of the trip was bonding with Judy. Every day, Judy and I would walk up into the hills, or along the water's edge, or downtown, discovering Chania's secrets.

Judy loved boats and sailing; it delighted her to see the little sailboats leaving the marina going out into the turquoise-colored Mediterranean Sea.

Chania was a similar size and feel to Rockport, Massachusetts (the town adjoining Gloucester), reminding us of home. We walked everywhere together, telling each other the stories of our lives. I got to tell her about my life with Mitch and feel the sadness and grief I desperately needed to feel. She too told me sad and happy episodes from her life. We walked and talked and cried and ate our way through the little town.

One especially cold and raw day, we stopped into our hotel restaurant where the waiter, Jonnie, a pleasant looking man, suggested we get the house soup, lemon fish stew.

As we ate the soup my sadness and grief subsided. I felt the warmth of the broth in my throat and was genuinely happy. I had forgotten what happy felt like and, for the moment, this was it. The next afternoon the sun was shining. It was five degrees warmer, and I wanted to feel happy again. We went back to the hotel restaurant and ordered the same soup from Jonnie.

After he brought the soup, he asked us, "Where are you from in America?" I responded, "I live in a small town outside of Boston called Gloucester." Jonnie stopped, got quiet, and said, "The only place in America I have ever been in is Gloucester!" Then I stopped. We all laughed.

When Judy and I returned home we had bonded so deeply that for many years she invited me to share dinner with her and her husband several nights a week. We became like family, and I felt so grateful for our deep connection that started on our trip in that little town in Crete.

My children had lost their father and now they wanted to spend time with me. I am grateful for that special time we had traveling.

### Bali—2013 with Sasha

Sasha had graduated from college a year after Mitch died. It was tough getting through that last year. But she managed and kept her grades up. After her graduation she decided to take time off to unwind and travel with some friends. While traveling in Southeast Asia they ran into bedbugs in Thailand.

From Sasha's reaction, I understood it was unsettling, perhaps even traumatic. She called me and asked if I would meet her in Bali. Bali had never been on my radar. I had never thought about going there, but when Sasha called, I immediately said, "YES." I knew she needed me and that we'd have a great adventure.

I went online, picked out a few Airbnb places to stay—one in Kuta, one in Ubud, and one in Candidasa—packed my bags, and got on a plane. We met up at Denpasar airport and from then on, we were together. The house in Ubud was my favorite. It was called Bijoux, located in the middle of a rice patty. It was made from antique, colorful hand-painted carved wood. It looked like a dollhouse. I was particularly taken with it. The flower in the front yard blooms for one day each year. We were lucky enough to be there when it bloomed.

Together, we developed an easy, daily routine finding a balance between doing self-care and educating ourselves about Balinese culture. Self-care consisted of yoga, biking, hiking, swimming, laughing, and getting massages (which were both fantastic and affordable). Our cultural education mostly involved going to Balinese Dance theatre, taking a few hiking/biking tours, and eating local Balinese food.

We learned about the workings of the Balinese Hindu family.

In America we have three meals a day—breakfast, lunch, and dinner, always served roughly around the same time each day. In Bali, the mother gets up at 5 a.m. and makes a large pot of rice, big enough to feed her entire family. She leaves the rice in the kitchen and when family members are hungry, they help themselves. They do not sit down together like we do in America. Their bellies are their internal clock, not a presupposed time when you're supposed to be hungry. They eat when they wish to.

Families live together in compounds. Instead of multiple bedrooms like an American home, in Bali they have several small buildings. The parent's building is higher off the ground, to show respect. There is a kitchen building, a temple, and burial ground. When a family member dies, they are placed out in the open air and given injections of embalming fluid until a proper funeral box can be made and enough bodies are accumulated for a cremation ceremony. After cremation, the ashes are scattered in the sea. The person's spirit is invited to return to the home temple and live on with their family until their next life. Again, it's a very different approach to death than we have in America. I was especially interested in the way in which the family had time with the body. In America, the dead body is immediately removed, like the death never happened. In Indonesia they have time to get use to the fact that the person has died. The body might be around the compound for as long as a month. Death is a common occurrence and everyone from the very old to the very young get to experience it. It was good for me to see this very different approach to how another culture deals with death.

I am also struck by the way they have structured long-term care for aging parents. We learned that the youngest son in a family is the chosen child to take care of the parents at the end of their lives, while the oldest son is free to do whatever he wants.

Sash and I looking at Mount Batur

Sasha and I stayed in Bali for almost a month. Traveling together worked for us. We became even closer, more connected. We learned how to listen and hear each other, creating a stronger, more compassionate relationship.

## Japan at last: April 2017
## with Noah and Sasha

"Mom," it was Noah calling early on a Sunday morning. "I'm so excited, Kyla and I have been talking about your birthday, turning 70, and I want to take you to Japan!" I am stunned, excited, touched. This is so unexpected and fantastic and unbelievably sweet. Noah continues in an excited voice, "Sasha wants to go, and Aaron feels badly, but there's just no way he can leave Westford right now with all his responsibilities. You've wanted to go to Japan since you were 10 years old, and this is the year to do it before Sasha starts nursing school and I get married. We'll make the time, let's go in April when the cherry blossoms are in full bloom falling like pink snow and Kyoto is at its most beautiful covered with layers of fragrant petals."

I am feeling so loved by my children. They know that I am fascinated by Japan, and they want me to experience it with them as my guides. Both Noah and Sasha have spent many years in Southeast Asia traveling, seeing the sights, and tasting the food. Neither of them has been to Japan, this foreign place I feel so connected to. Now we will all experience it together.

We arrived in Osaka around 8 p.m. Sasha and I are hungry, so we go out in search of food. Noah stayed in, getting much-needed sleep. The next morning I'm up at 6 a.m., ready to go. I don't want to waste a moment. I can't wait to experience Japan! When Noah wakes up, off we go in search of coffee. I had never heard that Japanese coffee was great, but now I am experiencing it and am happily surprised. Noah and I walk around and find "The Market" where they sell everything, mostly booth after booth of magnificent fish. We hurry back, wake Sasha, and return to the market to order lunch. Our picks are fresh, grade-A fatty tuna and scallops. The food is heavenly, so we order beer to go with it. When we return to our room hours later, we pack and get ready for our trip the next day by train and bus to Takayama where we will be staying at an Onsen Ryokan in the Japanese Alps for the next two nights.

A Ryokan is a traditional Japanese inn that features tatami matted rooms, communal baths, and kimonos. Onsens are the hot springs and facilities near them.

Noah and Sasha have planned this week with both rest and recreation in mind. We begin with rest. Meals are included and designed for us. We take several hot tubs and wear traditional Kimono to dinner.

Noah and Sasha are ready for anything, all dressed up in their kimonos.

I loved being in a country where every Onsen Ryokan has better bedding than my own fine bedding at home. The beds are so comfortable—human size, not too large, just right. After two days of baths, great meals, and many games of Gin Rummy, we are ready to see the rest of Japan. The plan: go to Tokyo and then Kyoto. Tokyo is fast and loud like New York City. There is a park, similar to Central Park. We visit shrines. And the children make jokes about everything including many about me whenever possible! There is much laughter and ease with each other.

Now we are ready for Kyoto. The Japan I have been waiting for. We rent bikes and ride them in the cherry blossoms just as Noah had promised. What joy!

The week has flown by. The kids need to leave and return to their busy lives. We had a last dinner in a great restaurant we happened upon. The chef turns us on to plum wine which has become a favorite of mine ever since. Noah and Sasha are returning home, leaving, and I am staying.

I had planned to stay in Kyoto for another 10 days. Another challenge, another "growth opportunity." As luck would have it, on my first day out alone, I found a bookstore with only one book written in English. It was Alex Kerr's, *Another Kyoto*. Perfect! From then on, Alex became my guide and companion teaching me where to go, what to look for, and how to see it. I spent the next ten days with Alex Kerr's book in hand. I walked so many miles in Kyoto that by the time I flew home my feet hurt so much I could barely walk. It was worth it.

cherry blossoms

For ten days, I walked around Kyoto alone in a trance as though I almost knew my way around the city, and yet I didn't. As I moved through Kyoto, I knew there were so many secrets still hidden from me. But one secret I discovered was that if you want to change something, you must change the way you perceive it. Give it a new status, as the monks did for the mud bowls, or as I have been doing for my life. Then believe in the transformation.

## Chapter 13
# Bittersweet Moments

*I am grateful to have loved and to have been loved.*

# Bittersweet

A bittersweet moment is one in which you are both happy and sad at the same time.

We had bittersweet growing in our yard in Gloucester. Mitch use to create what he called "a privacy screen" using our bittersweet.

# Bittersweet Moment #1

Mitch died when Sasha (our youngest child) was in their second year at Pitzer college, in Southern California. Along with going to classes, they were experimenting with life, relationships, and spent their junior year in Nepal living with a family and learning to speak Nepali. Sasha was 20, (about the same age I was when I lost my father) and was able to keep it together for the next two years, graduate with good grades, and end up with a college degree from an excellent college. We, the family, were very proud and keenly aware of how upsetting the loss of Mitch was. It was very sad he would not be at their graduation. It was a bittersweet moment. So, Sasha's two brothers, Aaron, and Noah, along with my brother Gene, and Mitch's sister Susan and I, flew out to California to celebrate Sasha's magnificent achievement.

**Footnote:**
When Mitch died in 2010, Sasha was on a journey of self-discovery. Sasha was transforming herself from female cis gender to transgender. Sasha would call and tell me about her changes. I didn't understand, it was too foreign an idea for me. Sasha would call again and again, lovingly explaining that she was becoming male. "Really," I'd say in a surprised voice. That conversation went on for a few years until finally, Sasha told me it was time for me to get it! She was getting angry at my inability to understand and accept it. It wasn't easy for me, but I wanted to learn and embrace it. I knew to keep our relationship a loving one I had to, and so I did. When I write about Sasha in those early years, Sasha was my daughter. Now Sasha has successfully become my son. Sasha is a beautiful, unique, exciting soul, and whatever gender they are, I love Sasha with all my heart.

## Bittersweet Moment #2

Emma was born three months early. She arrived weighing two-pounds six-ounces. She fit in the palm of my hand. Her doctors immediately put in a feeding tube to ensure she got nourishment four times a day. At five-and-a-half-years-old, her tube was removed. She started eating completely on her own and has ever since.

Emma has two grandmothers who both adore her but no grandfathers. Both Jim and Mitch died before she was born. Sometimes she'll say to me, in a strong Brooklyn accent (I have no idea where it came from) "Zayde (grandfather in Yiddish) Mitch DYIED". Mitch would have loved Emma as she would have loved him.

November 1, 2013

Dearest Emma,

It is November 1st today; you are now more than a month old. When you were born you weighed 2-pounds 6-ounces. You were so tiny. Your father's pinky finger was bigger than your leg. From the very first moment I saw you (you were only minutes old), I fell in love with you. I took one look and saw the strength and determination you have. I thought; *This girl is a tiger, she will be just fine.* Now, weeks later, you are fine.

Even though your parents are tired and over-worked, they both are happy, they both have broad smiles on their faces. You brought the smiles with you when you came. Emma, you are my first grandchild and I love you.

Baba

When you went to pre-school, your teacher asked all the kids what they wanted to be when they grew up. With no hesitation, you answered: "A Tiger."

## Bittersweet Moment #3

It was summer, a beautiful sunny day. Rain was predicted. We borrowed a tent. Neither Kyla or Noah (the bride and groom) was concerned. Their love, so strong, would make their wedding day perfect. And it was perfect—it really was perfect, except it wasn't exactly perfect for me. There was one problem. Mitch was not coming to his son's wedding. I knew he couldn't come—for me it created a bittersweet moment. I noticed a pair of Topsiders left under a white chair. I thought to myself, *Look, he did come, he left his shoes.*

## Chapter 14
# Finding Gulfport

*A* Soul Place *is a special site or spot*
*where we experience unique feelings*
*of belonging, empowerment, and*
*energetic rejuvenation.*

Mateo Sol, Lonerwolf.com

## Being in Gloucester

Being in Gloucester without you is like
eating a hotdog without mustard and sauerkraut.

is like: driving on the left side of the road.

is like: climbing a mountain in Flip Flops

is like: Kissing with your mouth wired shut.

it is Loving you Knowing you're never coming back.

W here do you go in the winter?" I ask everyone I know or bump into on the street. I have returned to Gloucester after being with Sasha in Bali. I can't seem to wear enough warm clothes or keep my neck out of the wind. It is not only the cold that I have returned to, but the loneliness of my home where I now live alone.

By the time the next winter rolls around I am booked to visit friends on the west coast of Florida: Sarasota, Venice, Sanibel Island, plus another small town my friend Jan told me about. She says it's a special little town; only 12,000 people and 30 percent are gay. I visit all the towns on my list, but I don't connect to any of them. It is only when I walk around the funky downtown of Gulfport that I feel at home, relaxed, and safe. I decide to rent a place the next year, 2014. I am smitten with this little town. It reminds me of being in my backyard in 1956 when I was ten.

The next year I rented a little house near town and met a realtor. We became friends. One morning I got an early call from April, "Kate, I have five houses to show you today. I'll pick you up at 10:00, okay?" I'm game, but really, I'm thinking to myself: *I can't buy a house. I live in Gloucester.*

*Can I really afford to buy a house?* April, true to her word, picks me up at ten and we're off looking at little bungalows in Gulfport. House number one holds no interest for me but as we approach house number two, suddenly I feel excited. The house is painted turquoise, a color I have never particularly liked, but in this sweet setting, it works.

When I walk inside, I am amazed that instantly I know this is my house. Is it the original wood floors or the perfect layout—two bedrooms, two baths, separated by a living room and dining area—or is it the garage where I can clearly see myself making a fabulous art studio? Instantly, I know it's mine.

I have never bought a house before by myself and I have no idea what I'm doing. I find myself overcome with sadness. It is caught in my throat, tears are forming...why? *Why isn't he here with me?*

Would he like Gulfport? I never would have found it with him. He never would have agreed to look at another house in another place. I wouldn't have needed it. I wouldn't have needed a new life because I was happy with the old one.

By coincidence, my neighbors in Gloucester also live in Gulfport. I trust them and ask if they would come look at the house. They agree. I thought they would be able to tell me if the plumbing was good and if the foundation was solid. They own several properties and are savvy Airbnb hosts. Tucker took one look at the house as well as the address and gave me a big thumbs up. "This is your house," Tucker grinned. "Look at the numbers—there are three 13s, and today is March 13th—three-13. It's yours."

I wasn't expecting Tucker to be superstitious. I thought he would bring logic and critical thinking to my lack of experience. But I knew he was right, it was mine. I made a bid, and it was accepted.

Gulfport has become my second home.

I take Tai Chi every Tuesday and Thursday. I belong to a serious writing group. Sometimes, when I'm feeling confident, I go to Swing Night at the Casino and dance or to hear live music. The group Hot Tonic is my favorite.

I ride my bike everywhere while listening to "Triplicate," Bob Dylan singing from the *Great American Song Book*

I use the house like a retreat house. Friends and relatives come to visit and work on whatever project they wish to work on. Or, like my cousin Paul, who just enjoys riding his bike and eating a fish taco at his favorite place, Little Tommy's Tikki. More than once, friends will ask how I found Gulfport. I say, "I don't really know. I came here and it was clear it was my place." Other people say the same thing. It is as if Gulfport chooses us rather than us choosing it.

## Mourning

Mourning has lifted
it is no longer the heavy woolen cloak
I wore each day
It is now an occasional wave
sometimes crashing on the shore
but mostly just slowly lapping up the sand

I have found that mourning is a trickster
a multi layered monster
I declare myself healed
Then I hear the celestial sound of Yo Yo Ma's cello
Instantly I am brought back to loss

My body remembers...
You are not by my side at the beach
You are not at the birth of our first grandchild
You are not on the other side of the bed

You continue to be missing
I have taken off the burdened woolen cloak
in it's place I wear my good nature.

I am human with an indomitable spirit
to continue
I am, Hi·Ne·Ni, here I am
until the monster comes by uninvited
for a quick visit, just to say hello,
and jars me back to you once again

## Chapter 15
# A Recipe for a Happy Life in the Time of the Corona Virus

**Birth • Friendship • Routine • Exercise • Laughter**

*Our highest calling in life is to thrive, and not just survive.*
*During this incredibly challenging time,*
*we must do our best to thrive.*

Donald T. Lannone, D.Div.

n March 2020, two important events took place. My grandson was born, and America was unwillingly dragged into the worldwide pandemic.

Arden Dutch Cohen was born on March 17th at 4:30 a.m.

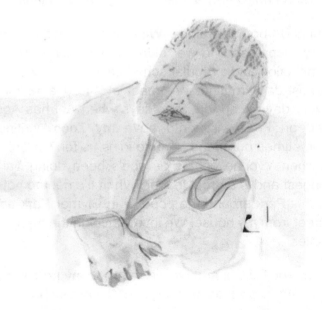

The birth went well, no complications. The next day his numbers were good, and after his circumcision, Arden and his new parents left the hospital and went home. Arden is a happy baby who thinks it's normal to have two parents home all day making sure he's happy, fed, has a clean diaper, and is always comfortable. The new little family is like cats, lying around sleeping, eating, and resting all day long.

The second event was the announcement that America was in a worldwide pandemic. President Trump was telling the American people not to worry about the Coronavirus—it would all be over very soon. It was "just going away," he said. At the same time his head scientist, Dr. Anthony Fauci, was warning Americans to take precautions, wear a mask, keep six feet apart, and stay home. We went into lockdown on March 18th.

When the pandemic first started, I connected with Ani, a woman I only knew a little from my Tai Chi class.

Ani and I both live alone. We quickly realized we could get very depressed if we didn't have some daily human connection and a regular schedule. Cleverly, we created an almost-daily routine. We meet at 11:00 a.m. for Tai Chi every day except on Thursdays when Ani has Aqua Yoga and on Fridays when I have my Zoom writing group. Sometimes our friend Yvonne joins us for Tai Chi. We love it when Yvonne comes as she's been doing Tai Chi the longest and is a great leader. When it's not too hot we walk in Ibis Park around the pond or in Clymer Park across the street from my house. We love watching the many birds and turtles.

After our Tai Chi routine, we return to my front porch where we each have a glass of gingerade kombucha.

# Tai Chi
## mind • Body • Spirit

We toast each other and enjoy more talk and insights into our past, present, and future. Ani and I have a lot in common. We both started our early lives in Queens, New

York and have discovered we know all the same show and pop tunes, often bursting into song on the spot. She has become my soul sister. Sometimes Bill, my next-door neighbor, joins us on the porch, sharing his thoughts about our current world. Often, we disagree in a friendly way.

The other important activity Ani and I have made a priority is watching the sunset almost every night together. And like the Beatles said, we "follow the sun," finding new places to watch as the Earth moves around the sun. Our latest place to watch is a little beach we have come to love, called Sunset Beach. Most everything Ani and I do together is free. The Beatles were right, "The best things in life are free."

For the time being, I am staying in Florida. Florida is now a hot spot with a grim rise in COVID-19 deaths. We are living with a hidden enemy we can't see or feel or touch. Hidden in plain sight, it kills people for not wearing a mask or for having a job as a caregiver in a nursing home or a worker in a meat packing plant. When I go to the grocery store (an essential reason to go out) I wear a N95 mask (a serious mask), gloves, and a hat.

I have noticed the clearing of the skies, less pollution so that the birds and the plants are happier and more productive. The birds always sang, but now in the time of COVID, they are singing louder, stronger, and longer. Or is it that I am quieter, more meditative, more aware of the natural world around me, less dependent on other people, and more available to notice the other creatures that share my world? After two months, I still had half-a-tank of gas in my car.

I am not yet joining large crowds of people in the street protesting. But I am 72, retired, with a steady income. I have food and a roof over my head. I am not worried if I will have a job in the fall or ever again. Instead, I am watching the news and seeing the stark reality that I live in a racist country. I am reading and educating myself, hoping to learn how to be a more conscious white person.

Every day I Zoom. Zoom has become the new way to gather people together while keeping separate and safe. I have three Zoom groups that I meet with regularly. A Sunday meditation group, my writing group, and the most serious Zoom which met every day at 3 p.m. for three months. It is no longer meeting because we met our goal and Jonathan Rosen came home.

Over 50 friends and relatives would meditate and pray every day for Jonathan Rosen, my cousin June's husband. Jonathan got sick with COVID-19 while working in a nursing home in New Jersey. By the time he went into the hospital, he couldn't breathe on his own and was immediately put on a ventilator soon after. Close to death, his doctors put him on an ECMO (Extracorporeal Membrane Oxygenation Machine) as a last resort. At that point, June being a pro-active dynamo, called everyone she knew. Remembering old friends from college—Cal Arts in California—as well as everyone she knew in New Jersey and all relatives from everywhere. Two amazing old friends took up the challenge and created "The Love Army," a group of 18 or so regulars making a commitment to show up until Jon came home. Tess, a natural shaman, created many scenarios for us to imagine healing Jon. For instance, one day we went into Jon's lungs and removed a blood clot.

David wrote our motto: "What we do here in this time is SIMPLE, SHORT, and CONCENTRATED. It is immensely powerful because we say it is so. Jon is doing well and fine, safe in our care. We work to keep this space available here every day because he is certainly going home. We have never seen it any other way."

76 days after Jon went into the hospital, he recovered and is now home with his family. This is nothing short of a miracle. And we believe between his doctors, the machines, and his Love Army, "he was always going home. We just didn't see it any other way."

From what I can tell, all my kids and their partners and children are coping well in this pandemic.

Aaron, Kate, and Emma are very careful and stay home. Emma and I FaceTime twice every week. We're making a *Welcome to the Family* illustrated alphabet book for Arden. Emma is doing all the artwork. (example)

## H is for Happiness

One morning early in the pandemic she said to me, "You know, Baba, I have a loneliness problem."

"I'm so sorry to hear that," I said as I thought, *This is amazing coming out of a six year old.*

A week later I asked Emma how her loneliness problem was going. She said without hesitation, "Baba, I have a toolbox and I figured out how to fix my problem. I went on Messenger Kid and now I play games with my friends every afternoon."

Sasha and Megan have decided they want to move to the northeast from Atlanta where they have been living while Sasha was in nursing school and transitioning from being female cisgender to becoming a *they*—the preferred pronoun for those who have transitioned.

Megan applied and got into an architecture master's program at UMass while Sasha got a great job in Brooklyn. They will have two homes, one in Amherst and one in Brooklyn, commuting back and forth. Luckily, they're both young and energetic.

Very recently, Arden's new life changed. His parents' maternity leave ran out. Noah and Kyla had to return to work. Luckily, they both can work from home. But with a five-month-old, they need help, so they hired a nanny. That was working really well until the nanny decided she wanted to move out of Philadelphia. Sasha is going to visit soon and can help for a week. Then Arden is going to daycare.

I want to figure out how to travel to Philly and help for a few weeks while his parents adjust to life with Arden in daycare. I think it's a rare opportunity for me to be so closely involved in Arden's life and get to imprint while he's still very young.

During that time, I hope to see Emma and her parents as well as Sasha and Megan. I have missed my children during this pandemic.

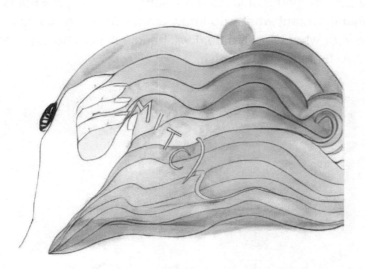

Ten years have passed since I first became a widow. Mitch and I had lived by the sea in a beautiful brown single house that we built together.

We raised our family there and lived surrounded by love. The love we had for our children, our families, our friends, and each other didn't die when he died. Instead, it continues to this day and gives me strength and support.

At present, I live alone in my sweet little house in Gulfport. It gives me great pleasure knowing I created a place of my own.

After years of therapy, writing, and travel, I have happily found myself. I am comfortable and confident. I know who I am, and I know what I like. Even the foods I eat are only foods I enjoy.

Family and friends come to visit here where it is warm and welcoming.

I have learned that life is a mystery. I don't know what is in my future, but what I do know is that whatever comes my way, or whatever I create, I will handle it. I will be okay, and more than that, I will thrive.

# Epilogue
# Beyond Widow: Living in the Light.

Mitch's birthday was on October 7. At the time I wrote this, he would have been 76 years old. One week later, on October 14, it was the tenth anniversary of his death. The morning of October 6 I woke up early. I wanted to honor Mitch for his ten-year anniversary. I wanted to put flowers on his grave and make it look beautiful. I wanted him to know he was "Forever Loved." But I was in Florida far away from his grave in Gloucester. Immediately I called Ruth. She was honored to be asked to help, and that afternoon Ruth and her husband Ed went to the cemetery and put beautiful flowers on Mitch's grave and sent me a photo.

After receiving the photo, I also wanted to put flowers on his grave, but I had to do it virtually. I added some bright orange tulips to my drawing of his grave and then superimposed that drawing onto the photo Ruth sent. Finally, I was satisfied. I felt I had contributed to the anniversary. Then a poem came out of me. And Sasha created a video of our earlier life with Mitch. Sasha posted it on Facebook. It became a celebration. The kids and I watched the video together the night of the 14th. We laughed, and of course, we cried.

Kate Seidman

When you become a widow

A widow

A widow

It's like you were wounded

Or shot

Or like you fell

Broke your hip

Your leg

Your arm

Your heart

When you become a widow, your heart is broken

You need to heal

# THE WIDOW ROADMAP

And it takes time

The person who would have taken care of you is gone

But you need love

You get it from relatives

Children

Friends

Eventually you heal

The wound becomes a scar

Sometimes painful, especially in the rain

Finally, the sun comes out

You go to the ocean

Sit with your feet soaking in the sea

and watch the sunset

Your scar begins to fade

Your friends comfort you

You start to sing and dance

And remember who you are

You start to thrive

You are a shooting star

You go to the ocean
sit with your feet soaking in the sea
and watch the sunset
your scar begins to fade
your friends comfort you
you start to sing and dance
And remember who you are

You start to thrive
You are a shooting star

# ∼∼∼Acknowledgments∼∼∼

I want to thank all my friends and relatives who have listened, looked, and "liked" this book from it's early conception to it's final finish ten years later. Thank you for loving me through it all.

Now to name you:

My children: Aaron & Kate, Noah & Kyla, Sasha & Megan
My Grandchildren: Emma & Arden
My Brothers: Dan & Gene
My Cousins: June Grushka, Linda, Joan, & Paul Lewis
My Sister-friend for 60 years: Sheila Groonell
My Publisher & new dear friend: Thea Rademacher

My dear friends from every part of my life:

Ruth Mordecai, Ani Crane, Yvonne Williams, Dale Rosen, Marla & Larry, Harriet Lerner, Nancy Goodman, Anita Pandolphi Ruckman, Claudia & Brent, Meryl Sheriden, Nancy & Jon Coppelman, Mo Pertik, Abbe Smith, Ilene Seidman, Ana Rogers, Diane Faretra, Loren Doucette, Andrew Widtfeldt, Arnie Kotler, Bill Corey, Mike Flood, Camilla Blackman, Susan Cohen, Robin Cohen, Deirdre Donchain, Mel Brown, Sally Plone, Lynda Danzig, Debbie Danzig Brodie, Joanie Black, Joseph Napolitano, Joanna Colwell, Tabitha Saletri, Juni Van Dyke, Michelle Barton, Pamela Gorden, Gisa Indenbaum, Barbara Oliver, Rosalie Harrington, Ronnie & Sonia Goplart, Alexandra Geiger, Laura Hayes. My Gulfport family! Tai Chi group, writing group friends, you know who you are... and how much you helped in the writing and drawing of this book! Laura Vance. Jennifer Lee Levits, Tucker & Leslie, Janet & Frank Sandie Horwitz, Lindsay Crouse, Michelle Barton, Jan Weinshanker, Judy Wright, Yhannah Coffin, Lisa VanSant, Stephen Bates, Jan Surrey. Thank you All ♥ Kate

# ABOUT THE AUTHOR

Kate Seidman graduated from New York University in 1970. After graduation, she drove across the country to California where she secured a coveted teaching position in the Berkeley Unified School District. She has taught art from third grade to the college level. Kate has had numerous business ventures, including a porcelain jewelry business, a silk painting studio and school, and a woman's clothing shop called The Art Room.

After the death of her beloved husband Mitch, Kate persevered and built a new life for herself. She now divides her time between the town where they raised their three children, Gloucester, Massachusetts, and her home in Florida.

www.kateseidman.com